WORLDWISE

SPACE

Written by
Nick Pierce

Illustrated by
Steve Wood

BOOK HOUSE
a SALARIYA imprint

This edition first published in MMXIX by
Book House

Distributed by Black Rabbit Books
P.O. Box 3263
Mankato, Minnesota 56002

Consultant:
Dr Stuart Clark holds a first class honours degree
and a PhD in astrophysics. He is a Fellow of the
Royal Astronomical Society and a former Vice
Chair of the Association of British Science Writers.
He writes the Guardian's "Across the Universe" blog
and articles for New Scientist, and is the author of
The Search for Earth's Twin.

Cataloging-in-Publication Data is available
from the Library of Congress

Printed in the United States
At Corporate Graphics,
North Mankato, Minnesota

9 8 7 6 5 4 3 2 1

ISBN: 978-1-912233-89-2

Contents

Introduction 4

The Solar System 6

Our Home Planet 8

Watching the Sky 10

Moons 12

People on the Moon 14

Working in Space 16

Space Probes 18

Timeline 20

Quiz 22

Glossary 23

Index 24

Introduction

When you look up into the sky you are looking into space. The Earth's sunlit, day-time sky looks empty, but at night-time you can see thousands of objects that are millions of miles away. At such huge distances the stars look like tiny points of light, and even galaxies with billions of stars are only faint smudges to us on Earth. But up close, the view changes. Space is full of potato-shaped moons, exploding stars, giant balls of gas, city-sized dirty snowballs that are too small to be seen from Earth, and much more.

On each spread you will have to look for different objects in the main picture.

The universe is everything: It's everything you can see, everything you can think of, and much, much more. The universe contains you and the planet Earth where we all live. It includes the solar system, the family of planets of which Earth is part, and the Milky Way galaxy, the massive star system in which our solar system is found. At vast distances are many millions more galaxies, each one moving further apart as the universe keeps expanding.

Can you find...?

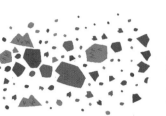

◀ Asteroids
Asteroids are fragments of rock and metal.
The asteroid Gaspra is about 7.5 miles (12
kilometers) across.

▲ Jupiter
Jupiter is the giant
of the solar system.
It is more than 11
times wider than
our planet, Earth. It
is made mostly of
gases and is known
as a "gas giant."

▲ Venus
Venus is the hottest
and brightest planet
in the solar system.
It is surrounded
by a poisonous
atmosphere.

◀ Mercury
Mercury is made of rock and is covered in
craters. It is the closest planet to the Sun. It is
scorching hot by day and freezing at night.

The Solar System

The solar system is the Sun and its surrounding family of planets, moons, asteroids, and comets. It was created out of a vast cloud of gas and dust. Most of the cloud's matter was used to create the Sun—the gigantic star at its center. At the same time it formed the asteroids and comets, many of which came together to form the planets and their moons.

▲Comets
Beyond Pluto, there are billions of comets. These giant space "snowballs" are made of ice, gases, rocks, and dust.

▼The Sun
The Sun is a hot spinning ball of luminous gas called a star. It is the biggest object in the solar system. The Sun's gravity keeps its family of planets together in space.

▶Earth
Earth is unique. It is the only planet we know of with life. Around three-quarters of its surface is covered in water.

Can you find...?

▲Balloon
People have traveled in balloons into near-space. In 2014, Alan Eustace reached a height of 25.73 miles (41.4 km).

▲Satellite
Satellites orbiting the Earth can collect information about our weather systems. They can also identify mineral deposits, crops, and movements of sea life.

Our Home Planet

Earth is unique. It is the only planet that we know of with life. Water covers around three-quarters of its surface, and it is home to millions of different life forms. The gases that form the Earth's atmosphere keep its surface temperature warm enough to support life.

▲Plane
Aircraft often fly in the stratosphere, the second layer of the Earth's atmosphere.

9

Watching the Sky

▲ **Modern telescope**
Telescopes based on Earth can look into space, as most light and radio waves get through Earth's atmosphere. Satellite telescopes reveal much more.

▲ **Constellations**
Constellations are patterns of stars that have a recognizable shape, sometimes of an animal or mythical creature. People once used these constellations to navigate.

Mayan

Hipparchus

◀ **William Herschel (1738–1822)**
Herschel was a British astronomer who built telescopes to study the stars. He discovered the planet Uranus in the process.

◀Fire
Can you find the fire in
this picture?

▲Mayan
The Mayans
were one of the
earliest civilizations
to study the
movement of
the stars before
the invention of
telescopes.

William Herschel

Telescope

▲Hipparchus
Hipparchus,
considered the
greatest astronomer
of the ancient world,
was Greek. He made
some of the earliest
accurate models of
the movements of
the Sun and Moon.

T he first humans simply used their eyes to
look up at the hundreds of stars in the night
sky. Those they called "wandering stars" we
now know as the planets. Today we use computer-
controlled telescopes. They are built high on
mountaintops, away from city lights and above the
clouds, to capture the clearest views. They look into
space and record what they see for us.

Can you find...?

▲Craters
Craters on the Moon are created by the impact of asteroids and other objects from space that have collided with the surface.

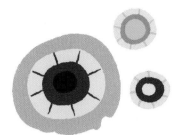

▲Satellite
Can you find this satellite in the picture?

Moons

There are 150 known moons in the solar system. They travel around their own parent planet, and all planets and moons travel around the Sun. Only Mercury and Venus have no moons. Jupiter has at least 53, including Ganymede, the largest moon in the solar system. The same side of our Moon always faces us as it travels around the Earth. The dark areas we see are lower and the brighter areas are lunar highlands.

▲Lunar module
Lunar modules were used by astronauts to land on the surface of our Moon.

People on the Moon

Can you find...?

▲Crater
How many craters can you count in this picture?

▲Lunar module
Can you see the lunar module in this picture?

▲Flags
The flags left on the lunar surface have faded and are now completely white.

O nly 12 men in history have walked on Earth's moon. The first successful Moon landing happened on July 20, 1969. Astronauts have since crossed 56 miles (90 km) of its surface.

◀Rock samples
Astronauts on our moon brought back over 880 pounds (400 kg) of rock.

14

◄Rocket
Can you see this rocket
in the picture?

▲Moon buggy
During the Moon
landings, astronauts
used lunar roving
vehicles or "moon
buggies" to explore
the Moon's surface.

▼Apollo 11
The Apollo 11
spaceflight was the
first to land men on
the Moon.

◄Astronaut
Can you see the Moon-walking
astronaut in this picture?

15

Can you find...?

Working in Space

There are now satellites orbiting the Earth where scientists live and work for months at a time. The largest is the International Space Station. It is so big that you can see it in the night sky.

▲ Spacewalk
Astronauts sometimes go outside the Space Station to make repairs.

▲ Weightlessness
There is a near-weightless environment aboard the Space Station.

◀ Experiments
Experiments in biology, physics, and deep space exploration are carried out on the International Space Station.

◀Astronauts
Can you find these
astronauts in this picture?

▲Solar panels
There are sheets
of solar cells on
the outside of the
International Space
Station. These
panels transform
solar energy into
electricity to power
the satellite.

▼Worker
Can you find this
astronaut working
on the satellite in
this picture?

◀Satellite
Can you see the satellite
in this picture?

Space Probes

Can you find...?

▲ Jupiter
The Voyager 2 space probe took pictures of Jupiter and its moons as it flew past the planet.

▲Nuclear power
Satellites that travel beyond Jupiter must rely on nuclear power instead of solar energy from the Sun.

Space probes are computer-controlled robots that investigate the solar system and deep space. These spacecraft often spend years circling other planets in our solar system and studying them up close with their cameras and scientific instruments. Without them, we wouldn't know much about Jupiter's colorful atmosphere, Saturn's rings, superfast winds on Neptune, or the many moons that orbit Jupiter and Saturn.

◀Mars rovers
Four "rovers" have been landed on Mars. They can move around and examine large areas of the planet's surface.

◄Camera

The cameras on the Mars rovers take pictures of the surface so scientists can study its color, texture, and contents.

▲Flyby

Space probes orbit planets and collect information about their atmospheres and surfaces.

▲Crater

How many craters can you count in this picture?

▲Moons

Can you find one of Jupiter's many moons in this picture?

►Mars landers

The lander space probes can send back pictures of the planet and examine soil samples.

Timeline

13.8 billion years ago
The Big Bang occurs and the universe comes into existence.

1942
The first German V2 rocket is launched 62 miles (100 km) from the Earth's surface (the edge of space). The age of space exploration begins.

5 billion years ago
Our solar system is first formed at this time. The Earth formed 4.6 billion years ago.

April 12, 1961

Yuri Gagarin becomes the first man in space. He completed one orbit of the Earth in his spacecraft, Vostok 1.

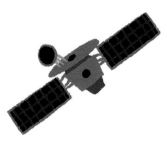

October 4, 1957

Russia launches the first ever satellite, Sputnik 1, into space

July 20, 1969

US astronauts Buzz Aldrin and Neil Armstrong become the first men to walk on the Moon.

21

Quiz

1. What is the name of the galaxy we live in?

2. What are asteroids made of?

3. Approximately how much of Earth's surface is covered in water?

4. Who discovered the planet Uranus?

5. Which two planets in our solar system do not have moons?

6. Which spaceflight was the first to land men on the Moon in 1969?

7. What is the largest manned satellite orbiting the Earth?

8. What space probe took pictures of Jupiter as it flew past?

9. What was the name of the first satellite ever launched into space?

10. Who was the first man in space?

Answers:

1. The Milky Way
2. Rock and metal
3. Three-quarters
4. William Herschel
5. Mercury and Venus
6. Apollo 11
7. International Space Station
8. Voyager 2
9. Sputnik 1
10. Yuri Gagarin

Glossary

Asteroid An irregular-shaped rocky body that orbits the Sun.

Atmosphere The layer of gas surrounding a planet or moon.

Comet A ball of rock, ice, and dust that produces a visible tail if it travels close to the Sun.

Crater A round hollow on the surface of a planet or moon.

Gravity A pulling force that holds everything together; stars in a galaxy, planets around a star, and objects on Earth.

Moon A rocky satellite that orbits a planet.

Orbit The path a planet or comet takes around the Sun, and the path a moon takes around a planet.

Planet A body of rock, or rock and gas, orbiting a star.

Satellite A man-made instrument like a telescope that orbits the Earth, or a moon orbiting a planet.

Solar energy Energy from the Sun, used to produce electricity and to power machines.

Star A spinning ball of hot, luminous gas.

Index

A
Armstrong,
    Neil 21
asteroids 6, 7,
    13, 23

B
Big Bang 20

C
comets 7, 23
constellations
    10

E
Earth 4, 5, 6,
    7, 9, 10, 13, 14,
    16, 20, 21, 23

G
Gagarin, Yuri
    21

H
Herschel,
    William 10
Hipparchus 11

J
Jupiter 6, 13,
    18, 19

M
Mars 18, 19
Mayans 11
Mercury 6, 13
moons 4, 7,
    11, 13, 14, 15,
    18, 19, 21, 23

N
Neptune 18

P
probes 18, 19

S
satellites 9, 10,
    13, 16, 17, 18,
    21, 23

Saturn 18
solar system
    5, 6, 7, 13, 18,
    20
space stations
    16, 17
Sun 6, 7, 11,
    13, 18, 23

T
telescopes 10,
    11, 23

V
Venus 6, 13